# A
# TEXAN
# IN
# TUSCANY

# A

# TEXAN

# IN

# TUSCANY

CASH NICKERSON

CNM Press
Austin, Texas

Published by

CNM Press
Austin, Texas

The net proceeds from the book will be donated to David's Cure, www.davidscure.org, the David H. Nickerson Foundation, which is dedicated to curing prostate cancer.

Cover and text design by Bookwrights

ISBN 978-0-9898009-0-7

## Dedication and Acknowledgements

*This book is dedicated* to all those who encouraged me to continue writing and "tasted" my stories as I drafted them. My new found "book friends" like Steve Bennett of Authorbytes, Marly Cornell who edited the text and really helped me understand the horizon expanding nature of my "journey," and Mayapriya of Bookwrights, who created the beautiful cover and helped me with formatting.

A thanks to all my neighbors in our wonderful Four Seasons Residences building in Austin, Texas who commented freely on my essays including the Wilkies, the Auerbachs, the Merediths, the Krasovecs, the Levinsons, and my in-laws the Thomases of Omaha.

And most of all to my wife, Evie, who supports or tolerates my Fabian tourist strategy—I still don't know which. And finally the Barrachi's and all the charming folks of Italy we met like Palio and our fellow vacationers.

The net proceeds from the book will be donated to David's Cure www.davidscure.org, the David H. Nickerson Foundation, which is dedicated to curing prostate cancer, the disease that killed my father and far too many fathers and grandfathers. David's Cure will then make a donation to the Siteman Cancer Center associated with Washington University in St. Louis. As you will read, my father inspired several of these essays and he is mentioned many times in this book.

# CONTENTS

# INTRODUCTION

**T**his book emanated from daily essay writing, a habit I acquired in Italy where an invisible muse visited me in the middle of a Tuscan storm. I have given my Italian muse the name of Maryella, our beautiful and smiling Sienese driver and tour guide. The essays are more or less in the chronology of a brief, but sensual, sojourn into Central Italy with my wife Evie.

While these essays were written in the nature of a travelogue, I make no attempt to provide a guide or roadmap. As you will learn, a "Fabian" is hard to follow. Fabian is a word I relearned as a result of my new writing habit. I use it here first to mean spontaneous as opposed to planned—opportunistic style versus a well-defined plan. The way the stories unfolded, however, did provide some history lessons. The early ones seemed to tug some childhood memories and meaning out of me. That could be because I was in the early stages of my writing life, or, perhaps, because I had never before been away for an entire week with my wife in our nearly thirty-two years of being hitched. Whatever the reason, the catharsis of the writing experience—though not easily described—was uplifting and enlightening.

As for accommodations, we stayed at Il Falconiere, outside of Cortona, for three nights, and then spent three nights about 25 kilometers from Firenze at Castello De Nero. Our final night was in Milan at the Park Hyatt next to the Galleria. All experiences were wonderful. The most unique, which surely helped me get started on my writing, was the seventeenth century family residence of Silvia and Riccardo Baracchi, Il Falconiere. As guests at the estate, we spent time with the proprietors and their other guests. Being there felt queenly familiar at the time, not rising to the level of déjà vu, but feeling more comfortable than such a faraway place should. Perhaps the then-strangers and now-friends we met there were all in search of the same meaning, and we connected because we were all somehow spiritually and emotionally in the same place. Or maybe special places draw special people. This requires further contemplation on my part—and that will come in time. But this feeling of interconnectedness led to an expansion of my understanding of the world that I feel both honored by—and compelled to share it with you.

Evie and I made up many words as we tried to speak Italian. My own personal favorite, I coined when wishing friends well: *Enjourno!*

# 1

# NO RUSH AFTER ALL

Fifty-something male, married thirty-one years, eight months, three weeks, and a day, in search of quiet respite and retreat with lovely wife/partner, from fast-paced, flat-out business and social life. Willing to travel, and willing to spend what is necessary. He loves wine and contemplative views—she loves art and wine. History a plus.

This is what David Norwood, our able travel guru from Highland Park, Texas, must have heard when he sent us to Tuscany for a week.

In full disclosure, I don't speak Italian, but my Spanish *"es perfecto."* I studied Spanish in school since eighth grade, and I saved enough money to turn seventeen in Madrid. Whenever I travel to Mexico or anywhere else in Central America, I insist that all engage with me *solamente en Espanol.* I have challenged myself to such a level that I seek to pass myself off as not American. I have been mostly unsuccessful in this endeavor, save once.

Evie and I were visiting Costa Rica, the northern portion where the Four Seasons is on the Playa Papagayo, just south of Nicaragua. I engaged an employee on the beach. I spoke only Spanish and avoided the characterization of "instant American." My hopes climbing, as we engaged in a fifteen-minute dialogue, I could tell from the look on his face that we had a breakthrough. I knew the moment of victory had arrived. I prepared myself for the trophy and award ceremony.

He smiled and looked me in the eye, and I knew we were language brothers.

He said, *"Italiano!"*

I was crushed. My heart sank. I had to ask, "Why?

Why? Why?"

And he said, "You speak Spanish like an Italian."

So, I have that going for me. My Spanish would get me through Italy.

It takes just shy of twenty hours to get from Texas to Cortona, a small village in Tuscany (Toscano). We flew from Dallas to London and then on to Roma (once you have been to Italy, you call Italian towns by their Italian names). Upon walking off the plane, we were met by an attractive assistant, Maryella. During our interchanges, she kept saying "*Pronto*," which means "hurry up" or "soon" in Spanish. So every time she said it, I tried to move more quickly. When she answered the phone, she would look at me (so I thought) and say "*Pronto*."

I decided Italy was a fast-moving place and might not be the place to relax after all. I was surprised. A friend had told me that—after he and his wife had lived in Venice for a year—they had to get out. Too slow! Repair service level agreements were measured in months, not hours, not days, not even weeks. And yet, "*pronto*" rang in my ears.

So I hurried. I moved faster and faster. *Pronto* meant hurry. *Pronto* meant now! We scurried off—now escorted by Maryella.

Later, well beyond Rome, I began to ask our driver about it. I told her to be honest with me if I was too slow. Just then, she answered her phone, "*Pronto.*"

I panicked and thought, *Oh no! I am too slow for Italy!*

When she hung up, I asked, ready to apologize, "What does *pronto* mean?"

It turns out that Spanish is not the same as Italian. "*Pronto*" does not mean hurry in Italian. *Pronto* means "ready," as in: I am ready to speak, I am ready to listen.

Upon arriving at Il Falconiere (the falconer), the world stopped. The pace was not a pace at all. The reason, I suppose, that landscapes are easy to paint is that you don't have to tell them to sit or stand still. And now, delightfully, we found ourselves simply part of the landscape—which has a universal language—stillness.

*Pronto.*

# 2

# THE TEXAS TUSCAN

Never underestimate the value of being underestimated. Texans, when it comes to knowledge and sophistication, often are. When I moved to Texas ten years ago, several friends, some from San Francisco and some from Chicago, said they had no intention of coming to Texas to visit me. I would need to come to them. It was not out of a knowledge of Texas itself, but out of a perceived stereotype that combined something like Daniel Day Lewis' character in *There*

*Will be Blood*; our former president, George W. Bush; and either John Wayne in any western or James Dean from *Giant*—or my personal favorite (as I am partially named after the character), a young James Garner, starring as an oil baron in *Cash McCall*. A slight accent and doubling or tripling the syllables in any given word, topped off with a liberal use of select Texas phrases, such as "fixin' to," "I reckon," or "y'all," will get you started down the road a pace. Add a swagger to your walk, and tell someone to "have a blessed day," and you can get a Texas brand on your hide.

The minute you answer the second question asked of you by anyone in Tuscano, "Where are you from?"— if it includes the state of Texas—you are a combination of the above-named characters, which they amalgamate into a larger-than-life statue the size of Firenze's prized possession, the seventeen-foot David. They immediately assume you are in oil.

On my first day at the magical place in the hillsides, walking distance from Cortona, when checking in at Il Falconiere, proprietor Riccardo Baracchi asked me where I was from. As soon as I mentioned Texas, he stood taller, nodded, and said "petrol."

I couldn't resist nodding assent, for several reasons.
First, I could tell it was significant to him. And, as it
would turn out, he would have stories to tell about what
I began to be called while there, "The Texas Tuscan."
Second, trying to describe my work in the aerospace
engineering recruitment business was way too complicated. And I was pretty sure that to fully disclose that I
was a business and negotiations lawyer (a deal maker)
would not get me the best seat at the table, or the best
wine in the cellar.

Third, it was not a lie anyway. I did own the min-
eral rights to our suburban home in Southlake, and
I did have a natural gas lease for my acre. I had once
done a deal for four acres on behalf of the homeowner's association there—so I do have experience at what
Texans would call being a "land man." And I was a
good landman, having obtained, for my neighbors and
me, a $25,000 bonus payment for a two-year lease, with
a two-year option and 25 percent royalty on the eve of
natural gas plummeting. (I had the luxury of playing
three firms off against each other and having good tim-
ing. Sometimes you just have to put people in a room
and see what happens.)

So, I was not an oil baron—never said I was. It was only a "stretcher," and not an outright lie.

As I was a bona fide Texas oil man, I asked Riccardo if he wanted to sell his stunning villa and estate. He laughed boisterously and said I could buy it all, his whole life and everything, including his wife Silvia. Neither Silvia nor Evie seemed to worry about that, both rolled their eyes—one clockwise, one counterclockwise. While you may find it strange that I noticed this, I was watching carefully to see if either of us would be smacked—not that I felt I deserved anything—but if Silvia slapped Riccardo, I might have gotten a slap just for good measure, or because I led him into it. The ladies chose instead to treat us like the children we were, and we were enjoying being children at that time, at that place.

Trying to understand the label of a bottle of Italian wine was, I am sure, where I lived up to the Texan Tuscan label the most. Evie and I lived for seven years in the San Francisco Bay Area and made frequent visits to the wine country. Buying California wine is easy. The bottles are smartly named by the grape that predominates the juice in the bottle. You buy a Chardonnay, you get Chardonnay grapes. You buy Cabernet Sauvignon, you get Cabernet Sauvignon juice. French wine bottles, I can figure pretty well, as they bear the region they are from. A Burgundy, whether red or white, comes from Burgundy. A Bordeaux comes from Bordeaux. Champagne comes from guess where? And it is pretty easy to learn that Burgundy reds are Pinot Noir grape juice.

But to read an Italian label, I am still not sure what it all means. They blend grapes I have never heard of. And Sangiovese is a different grape in different regions. I still don't know what Brunello means. But I do know that if a wine is from Monticelena, a small wine region in Tuscano, and has that on the bottle, it has to be 100 percent purebred Sangiovese grapes from that region. And, it is also called Chianti Classico, maybe Reserva, also.

I just couldn't figure it out. So, when ordering, I would just give a look like I imagined one of my true Texas oil buddies would, and the locals would put it in easier terms. I do warrant you, I have multiple degrees and high octane education in my tank; but between the jet lag, the language barrier, and the Chianti—well, suffice it to say, I did justice to my role. They would

finally take pity on me and just give me what was best.
As this was a restaurant problem, I could cope with it,
as dinner only came once a day.

Evie and I visited several wineries. In the company
of experts, and in the tasting environment, I did much
better and learned quite a bit. Antinori's new winery,
about ten minutes away from Castello Del Nero, was an
awesome sight. The winery is enormous and is layered
into the hillside about 25 kilometers outside of Firenze.
It is a beautiful, natural-looking structure with futuristic
tendencies. Inside is a series of barrel-shaped cathedrals.
A Texan might call it a "wine shrine." You truly feel like
you are in a barrel. We did a tasting in a cantilevered
balcony overlooking a production area. I have never seen
anything like it in California, or anywhere else.

The winery had an Antinori museum. His new
headquarters and all production was moving there.
While I'm used to thinking that most things are bigger
in Texas, Antinori's was the biggest winery I have ever
seen—and I am fixin' to head there for its first crush in
the fall.

The Antinori winery is so big, and so over the top.
The ceilings must have been five or so stories high and

had the appearance of wine barrel staves. The experience made me feel like a small Pinot Noir grape in a barrel. I thought that Marchesi Antinori could be the villain in the next James Bond movie, maybe as an evil guy trying to corner the wine market. While Marchesi Antinori is a highly respected patriarch, he had that look of the centuries-old landed gentry of Europe. And, as with all Bond villains, the antagonists think and live large.

Once you get a nickname like the Texan Tuscan, it becomes an obligation of sorts to maintain for the sake of those who gave it to you, who feel they have earned the entertainment rights. I did not disappoint the Toscanos or my fellow Americans, none of whom let on that I lacked the hat, buckle, and boots to properly play the role.

I do own those items, and recall debating about whether or not to bring along on this trip the Stetson and Lucchese classics I picked up at Allen Boots in Austin. And I surely reckon I will, the next time I am fixin' to head that way. I hope y'all join me and have a blessed day.

# 3

# GOT MILK, GOT GOD

Vacationers, as we were in Tuscano, are interlopers, invading and observing the life of others like one watches a rose bloom. Even a good vacationer is somewhat of a cross between a hobo, a gypsy, a vagabond, and a wanderer stealing energy, meaning, and life to transport in our memories, stories, and photographs back to our own rooted life places. May God forgive us our presumptiveness as we observed the environment, people, and landscapes as if it

were our right. And God bless those who gave us the
gift of a glimpse of the simplicity that was once all of
ours to savor. We were not always consumers; we were
all farmers and humans once.

If you obey your senses, all of them, not just sight,
that single overly reliant sense, you can experience Tuscano to its fullest. The scenery seduces the sight sense,
so you might need to close your eyes and open your
nose and ears, and touch everything you can. I closed
my eyes while at Il Falconiere, resisting the tempting
view of the verdant valley below.

Out of my left ear, I heard a cock crowing. Some
bird cooing I did not recognize was to my right; and the
sound of the wind through the trees circled around my
head, varying its decibels like an expensive Bose sound
machine. If I could identify a single smell, I would share
it with you now in writing. But imbibing the scents
of the Tuscan landscape was just like divining wine.
Some have a knack for this. They smell pears, cherries,
apricots, and even leather. If I was forced to discern the
scents of that early May day, I would pick lavender first
as paramount, followed quickly by moist, earthy green-

ery, a hint of rose, and a background of wet limestone and farmer's earth.

Riccardo Baracchi had spent the morning in his fields pruning grape vines on the day we arrived. When we met him, his wife Silvia was unimpressed with the evidence of farm work on his shoes. She said, "Look at the farmer's shoes," pointing out the mud and dirt of various grades on his shoes.

I mean no disrespect to the wives of the world, but I do wonder where they get the training to know just how to deflate a spouse in the company of others. We are proud of the mud on our clothes, and the dirt on our shoes. Maybe we don't help with the wash? Farm work is dirty work and hard work, I don't care what you are growing. Wine makes us so much happier than corn and beans, so there is a glamour factor with growing grapes. But make no mistake about it, it's farming. And it's gritty. Pruning is hard work and done by hand. Riccardo remarked that every crop of guests includes at least one person who wants to help with the grapes, but they never last more than five minutes in the field. Must be a bucket list thing.

From the ages of eleven to eighteen, I spent my summers working on my mother's family's farms in rural Minnesota. There were two primary farms, Uncle Duke's and Uncle Ted's, one outside of Hutchinson, and one outside of Litchfield. My uncle, Ted, by way of being married to my mother's older sister, had taken over my grandfather's farm. His name was Herman, but we just called him Grandpa.

Uncle Duke, Herman's son, had struck out on his own and had a substantial spread for that time and place. In addition to growing massive acres of corn, he had feedlot cattle and more pigs than I could count (and math was my strong suit). Uncle Ted had milk cows and some land, and some pigs and cattle, and even a handful of chickens. Milking cows is a tough way to go through life. But the weekly check from the farmers coop (when they came to drain the milk bulk tank of the white treasure each week) provided a hedge against the vagaries of weather and the havoc it could bring on a farmer's livelihood.

Whether you grow corn, beans, or grapes, farming is a humbling business. Those who engage in it tend to avoid atheism and hold strong beliefs in the powers of a higher power, God himself. In Cortona, that ancient walled village in the rolling hills of Tuscano, the evidence of that belief is apparent with the abundance of churches, monuments to saints, especially Santa Margherita, and a large, castle-like structure partway up or down the hill (depending upon your point of view) that, upon closer inspection, was a set of mausoleums, vaults, and crypts honoring and holding the remains of the departed, but not forgotten.

We spent some time on our way up the hill one day surveying the final resting place of the denizens of Cortona from the mid-1800s, or so, forward to present times. There were hundreds of crypts and tombs. Each had two unexpected accoutrements: fresh flowers and pictures that looked new and recent. And these emblems were not confined to the recently departed, but to those whose souls had escaped their bodies over 100 years ago.

My farming relatives were deeply religious and prayed a lot. They prayed for rain for corn, but only after it was planted and not when they wanted harvest. They prayed for a dry spell when they needed to cultivate or otherwise tend to the crops. They prayed

for warmth, but not on the days we were going to bail
hay or straw. And they prayed for good crops and good
health for animals who had quick life cycles. We prayed
before every meal and gathering. We prayed in church
on Sunday mornings and Sunday nights and even, for
good measure, on Wednesday nights. We said prayers
before bedtime and asked for good rest and sunshine,
or rain, depending upon what we needed.

We all had to learn what weather patterns and
different cloud types were. We watched the sky like
sailors. A gray morning was bad if we were to do field
work the next day, but a beautiful red sunset was a
great omen. You couldn't be good at prayer if you didn't
understand the weather—you had to know what to
pray for, and when.

The religious roots run deep in Cortona. According
to ancient Greek historians, Noah found this area 108
years after the flood. One of his sons discovered and
lived on that hillside that is now Cortona, the third-old-
est village in all of Italy.

The saint who protects it, fittingly, looked after us.

Margherita ran away from her village with a noble-
man who took her to his castle only to be his mistress,

it turns out. She found him murdered one day in the forest. Already an outcast in her own village, and now an outcast with her benefactor deceased, she came to Cortona and entered the order of St. Francis. Ultimately canonized by one of the Pope Benedicts, you can find her remains in Cortona. She is the saint who watches over the hobos, the reformed prostitutes, the gypsies, the wrongly accused, and, I like to think, the vacationers.

# 4

## SAY HELLO TO PALIO

I f you are lucky, you have had those in your life who have left you with "scenes" that you store in a library in your head. I believe we all can and do access these "scenes" when we need them, replaying them like movie clips. I have such a clip from 1996, a few months before my father died. We were walking together on a beach outside of San Diego, where my father, having overcome his initial educational disadvantage, was a professor of computer science at Point Loma Nazarene College. As best I can recall, it was Pacific Beach.

I cannot do justice to describing my father in an essay, but he had overcome great adversity, having been orphaned by a court and abused in a foster home. He ran away from that unhomely home in Indiana to Chicago where he survived as a street urchin until he was able to lie his way into the Korean conflict at seventeen, a year before his eligibility.

He never talked about his medals and missions in the Air Force (I found them once in a drawer). But on driving vacations, he would let me sit up front and be copilot and tell me what to say. It was a blast. We pretended to have a tail gunner and bombardier. When he needed a map, I got to be the navigator and the copilot.

He had only finished the eighth grade; and while he went on to achieve multiple degrees, he was an intellectual without them. Consistent with this ability, on that particular day, he asked a simple question. This was his hallmark, asking that profound question that was below the surface and forced you to go deep. "Why did we ever leave the beach?" He didn't mean me and him, or our family. He meant "us," "all of us."

When my father asked a question like that, the worst response was a quick one. If you decided to blurt out the first idea that came into your head, he would follow with another deeper challenge, or say, "Interesting, why don't you spend another minute thinking about it?"

All this was as if to point out that he had given you a diamond ring, and you treated it like something out of a Cracker Jack box. Why did we leave the beach? I remember surveying the Pacific Beach area. There were cute young girls in bikinis, surfers, fishing vessels, sailboats, and the fresh smell of the sea. Its mist and the cadence of waves were interrupted by the cacophony of sea gulls.

I recall seeing those that clearly had not left the beach. They were evident. They were working. They were manning the boats, giving scuba and surfing lessons, serving food in the restaurants, cleaning the beach, operating metal detectors, and fishing. I wondered about my father's question, but did not answer him. I stored the "clip" for another day.

In Cortona, as there seems in every Italian village, there are squares. If you make the trek up the steep hillside and enter the walled city of Cortona, you will find a square about a quarter mile straight up the hill.

This square looks exactly like the Austin Lyric Opera set of *Pagliacci*, with a church, some shops and restaurants, and people milling about. Narrow streets extend out from the square like arteries and veins from the heart. They are not straight, and they flow randomly, once leaving the square.

In fairness and upon reflection, the square isn't square, either. Having a choice to enter the church or a wine shop, I selected the latter, but not out of disrespect. While there is more wine exported out of Italy than any other country, from my brief experience, there were more churches than wine shops. The wine shop proprietor's name was Palio.

Palio told me about the village and explained the Tuscan wine regions to me as we tasted our way through them. He had been born a few blocks away, in the next square up the hill. His English was flawless, and his knowledge of the city a national treasure. I asked him whether Cortona was affected by World War II.

His face transformed as he began to answer the question. "There are two great days in our recent history," he began. He proceeded to tell me how Saint

Margaret had saved the village from the Germans. On the day that the Germans were to bomb Cortona, the patron saint of the city covered it in fog, and the Germans bombed a neighboring city instead. The other great time for the city was the American liberation.

I bought a case of wine from him for shipping to Texas, including a 2010 Sassicaia, an expensive Cabernet from Tuscano that could not be touched for at least seven years. If you recall the movie, *Sideways*, this is the wine that turned on Virginia Madsen's character, Maya, to wine.

Palio asked if we wanted a reservation for lunch. We said yes, but saw no phone. He walked outside and yelled across the square. "*Quattro por Una.*" We had just gotten a reservation for four at one o'clock.

We had two tour guides for Siena: Fabio and the aforementioned Maryella. Maryella was full of stories and always knew where we should go and what we should see. She was in the process of buying the fifteenth century house and tied her house into stories about Sienna. She had her own talent at connectedness as she wove the gate that was not up to code at her house to a gate in Sienna. It was as if her tour was a pneumonic device to help her in her meeting with inspectors later that night.

Fabio's father and grandfather had a shop off of the shell-shaped Piazza del Campo. Fabio still lives within walking distance from where he was born. Maryella and Fabio both told of the importance of Siena and how it was larger and more significant than Paris until the Black Plague (in the fourteenth century) decimated it. And later, the Spanish aligned with the Duchy of Florence and conquered it. But their pride and their history focused on the 400 years of greatness when it was the Republic of Siena.

Like Palio, Maryella and Fabio had a view of their city that you don't find on the Internet—they had stories that are more fascinating than Etruscan historical dates. They talk of conquerors in villainous tones. Where has our sense of this kind of history gone? Is the Internet turning history into a nothing more than a dry read—a list of factual begats, but no texture, no life? Are resources like Wikipedia an evolutionary step backward?

Sorry, now I sound like my father's son.

I have spent quite a bit of time thinking, speaking, and writing about mobility and its importance in modern human commerce. That subject was the foundation of my first book *StagNation*. The book was about the cascade of economic troubles that started in the US with the burst of the real estate bubble in 2008. Here in Cortona, families live where they have lived for hundreds of years.

But I have a renewed respect for those who stay at the beach. These are the guardians of our true history as a people. These are the folks who enrich us as we wander the streets and peruse the sights of places we barely touch.

God bless Palio. If you visit Cortona, say hello to Palio for me. You will find him in the wine shop in the square. And wherever your travels take you, to the beach or to the square, take heed from Aristotle, who advised in *Nicomochean Ethics*, "Treat people as an end in themselves, not as a means only."

These are not locals or townies existing for the service of vacationers. They are those people who stayed at the beach, the keepers of true history. They know the real story and remain the keepers of the treasures of our past. And now recalling my father's love for Aristotle, I wish he were alive so I could answer his question from 1996. It took me seventeen years, and meeting Palio, to get there.

# 5

# ODE TO PEDDLERS, A TEAR FOR CLAUDE

No matter what power your personal telescope and microscope, as you gaze at the sculptures and other artistic treats of Tuscano, whether man-made or divinely developed, you will have difficulty "cropping out" the peddlers. The sculptures, the squares, and the *duomos* attract them like cracker

crumbs attract ants. They seem to reproduce like rab-
bits. They wield many wares from replicas of David to
T-shirts that simply say "I Love Siena" or "I Love
Firenze."

It would be easy to view and treat them as they
have always been treated—or, shall I say, mistreated:
as outcasts, as street urchins, as peddlers, gypsies, and
hawkers. You can sense the disdain of the typical tourist. But I submit that to the extent we despise them, we
despise ourselves. As we look down on them, we look
down upon ourselves. As we thank our lucky stars we
are not them—the stars know better. From the per-
spective of the heavens, we are all peddlers, or we have
made our way supporting and living off those who are.
Peddlers, like most species, gained their dark reputation
from the worst of them, not the best of them.

As we made our way from lunch poolside on the
hills above Firenze at Villa Cora (Our thanks to the
Auerbachs from Austin) to the Piazza del Michelangelo,
a beautiful uphill then downhill stroll of about thirty
minutes, we enjoyed unobstructed views from above
one of the most incredible cities I have ever seen. As
we approached the former resting place of the beloved

David, which has been replaced by a replica, which appears to do justice to the original, we were accosted—not aggressively, but passionately—by peddlers of all shapes and sizes. They smiled, asked if we were American, spoke perfect English, and showed us their wares. If we said no, they left us alone. They were well mannered, polite, expressive, and they seemed to love their wares and talking about the details. The artists speak of their inspiration and how they painted the scene, how the light was just right that day, but you can't count on that again. You may see commodity, but they transform it to a rare earth metal.

Crossing the bridge known as Ponte Vecchio, we found it lined with little gold jewelry stores. While I at first found this gauche, I later learned that before there was gold, there was meat and guts and blood and butchers—the remains of which were thrown into the river below, producing putrid and indescribable odors. I prefer the gold.

My father's name was David. As I mentioned earlier, he was orphaned by a court, I believe, at the age of eight. While, nowadays, a failure to provide your child with a four-wheel-drive stroller with rear view mirrors can land you in trouble with Child Protective Services, in the 1940s, it was difficult, I understand, to sever parental rights.

While I met each of my father's parents, separately —my supposed biological grandfather and grand-mother, I had no desire to see them further. Upon hear-ing of my father's father's (Claude) passing, I didn't shed a tear for him. Claude would show up intermittently when he needed money, and my father would give it to him.

I remember once, down on his luck, he showed up in Upstate New York in an old beat-up Cadillac. The car was a mess, and the backseat was covered with adult magazines. I did have a chance, I now admit, to make absolutely sure that was what they were. I was seven-teen, and that's what we did. He was in his sixties at the time, I would guess. My father said his father had been married seven times, although not always needing a license. I doubt there is much of a record of his mar-riages and divorces.

My father never discussed the years he lived with Claude, and I never asked, except he would describe him as an entrepreneur, a charming entrepreneur, and

an inventor. My father said Claude invented a shampoo
of sorts, and he sold it door to door. Like a good father
would, Claude sometimes took his son, my father, to
work.

And my father was not there just to watch, but to
play an important role. In between each house, Claude
would dirty my father's hair with whatever he could
find or had with him, grease, oil, tar, or just plain mud,
depending on the circumstances and weather. Claude
would then convince the homeowner to let him prove
his concoction's effectiveness by washing my father's
hair in their sink. My father said that, because he was
along and Claude was so charming, they sold enough
shampoo to support the family.

My father was completely bald. On more than one
occasion, he blamed Claude's elixir. I don't know the
years exactly, but I would guess this was 1939 or so, as
my father was born in 1934, and gone from that "home"
by 1942. As best as I can tell from the whispers I have
heard, I believe there were many children, including
sisters and brothers and half-sisters and half-brothers.
And when Claude mobilized for a new territory with a
new woman, he left another helpless crew alone, and

the state picked them up as wards. The story tempers my libertarian tendencies.

American history, as told through plays, musicals, and movies, is replete with peddler characters. If you like plays, I refer you to Arthur Miller's *Death of a Salesman*. Spend an afternoon with Willy Loman and his son Biff. If you are partial to musicals, find the *Music Man* on Hulu or Netflix. Tell me you would not have bought a musical instrument from Professor Harold Hill who graduated from a nonexistent class at a conservancy that, unfortunately for him, did exist. Even the fact-checking Madame librarian fell in love with him. And finally, who can forget the peddler in *Oklahoma*, Ali Hakim, as he brought wares to Oklahoma from the "Far East." He was a ladies' man as well, as peddlers tend to be. Played by Eddie Albert, eventually of *Green Acres* fame, his peddler life ends when he winds up on the wrong side of Gertie's father's shotgun and settles down.

Maybe I have been too hard on Claude. My father forgave him; why shouldn't I? He settled long enough to become my father's father, and I suppose I am a product of a peddler's brief respite between territories. And hopefully, a first rate peddler myself, along with many of my best friends, I will bring to the "profession" what is the best of us, so future generations will be kinder to the peddlers in the hills of Firenze and around the squares of Tuscano.

I can now shed a tear for Claude.

# 6

## OF FARMING AND MARRIAGE: SUSTAINABLE AND ORGANIC?

My father, who was married until he died, said marriage was invented by people who had short lifespans. His sarcasm wasn't lost on any of us—including my mother. But he was a loving father and husband, and he led by example. My mother's family consisted exclusively of immigrant farmers. She herself grew up on a farm, the daughter of farmers whose parents were farmers in Europe. As I have said, I spent some time with that way of life during summers in the 1970s, before Monsanto altered the genetic makeup of plants and crops.

One of the most evident and visible scenes in Tuscano are husbands and wives working together at the winery, in the vineyards, in the villas for rent for those on holiday, and in their gardens. They seemed neither happy nor sad, didn't seem to care much about technology, and reflected a satisfying "working state" while they went about the rituals associated with farming. You could tell they practiced a farming style that would make Whole Foods proud, and the most activist agriculturalist in Austin take note.

Cortona sits on an intimidating hillside (Etruscans loved to build on steep slopes). As Il Falconiere was closer to the nadir of the alluvial plain known as the Val a Chiana, getting to the Etruscan walled city meant climbing the hill.

On the first day, we had asked folks at the villa about walking to Cortona. They laughed. But when we said, "No, really," they said it was about two or three kilometers, but it was straight uphill, and probably not a viable walk. They suggested we let them call a cab.

But Evie and I decided we could make the walk. So we asked for directions, as we had recalled the windy roads that had confused Maryella, our Sienese driver.

As we walked out of the Baracchi estate, we encountered stone houses along the street, most of which seemed to sit on at least an acre, maybe two, of land that was tillable and, indeed, was tilled. The look couldn't be more different than the suburban lawns of American cities, like my own childhood plot in Forest Hills, Pittsburgh. But it made me wonder whether the yards and grass we played in, which were worked by TruGreen and layered with chemicals from Home Depot, were to remind us of our agrarian roots. In those suburbs so uniform that they are nameless, a common sight was a young father on his John Deere riding lawnmower trimming the overly green, uniform, weedless and lifeless suburban grass.

In the acreage surrounding the villas and houses of Cortona, you find husband and wife, and sometimes their parents as well, working the land by hand, and shoulder to shoulder. There didn't appear to be anyone in charge; they all seemed to know what to do.

On the streets of Cortona, in the shoulders and ditches adjacent to the streets, there was no litter. Everything seemed to be something useful. There were no signs of waste and lots of signs that sustainability had never stopped here in Tuscano. There were objects that looked like compost barrels, and woodpiles for sticks picked up from the yard (which in suburbia we would put out with the grass clippings for Waste Management to pick up twice a week).

Chimneys had a light smoke coming from them, which didn't burn artificial logs, but rather parts of the tree that had been felled by a storm a couple years ago. For all of our study of sustainability and organics, it seemed that, rather than reading books, those interested in the subject simply needed to take a step backward in time and come to a place that has avoided some of our questionable progress of recent years.

Farming and marriage, according to some, go together like a horse and a carriage, and they developed together. Somewhere around 10,000–12,000 years ago, we "migrated" from a lifestyle of hunting and gathering to a life of domesticating plants and animals. This change is credited with much of human progress. Now we could feed more folks, and not everybody had to spend their days scavenging. Raising domesticated goats was sure easier than trying to find one, and finding berries compared with growing olives? One might fairly ask, "What took us so long?"

Of course, to work a farm you needed offspring. There is substantial evidence that families grew to support the work. There are some who argue that farming was the beginning of social classes (once you could store things of value, you had wealth). It allowed for the advancement of the arts, and led to innovation—the need for better tools of the trade. After all, if Mozart had to find his own food, forget about piano concertos—maybe he would have led the humming as a hunter and gatherer.

But all progress has its downside, and farming has its critics (both scientific and nonscientific, perhaps instinctively), which seem to be growing and buzzing in a "hive" type of way. If you haven't heard of the paleo diet, you have been living, well, in the Stone Age.

There are new scientific studies and evidence that

show that hunters and gatherers lived healthier and longer lives than we previously thought. The introduction of farming led, in fact, to a shortening and fattening of humans—farmers are not triathletes. Toward the end of the Ice Age, hunter/gatherer men were five-feet-nine, and women were five-feet-five on average. By 3000 BC, several thousands of years after agriculture started, average heights dropped to five-feet-five for men and five feet for women. Preagricultural longevity was twenty-six years, and post was nineteen years.

Some paleopathologists argue that farming was actually an evolutionary step backward. And many doctors endorse the paleo diet. You can find specialized paleo diet packages in stores like Snap in Austin, Texas. Sprinkle in some hatred for Monsanto's genetically manipulative work, calculate the impact on the climate of the extensive herds of beef and sheep, and you have to admit that farming is under fire worldwide.

Traditional marriage is under fire at the same time. Divorce rates continue to be high—50 percent for first marriages, 60–67 percent for second marriages, and the third time is not the charm with a 73–74 percent divorce rate. The first-time marriage age is at an all-time high: 28.7 years for men and 26.5 for women.

With our stagnant economy and endless recession, who has the resources to commit to support each other? Lacking the ability to work "shoulder to shoulder," whether on a farm or in an office, and the rise of work-place policies designed to ferret out relationships, it is no wonder marriage is being deferred and its usefulness debated. I have noticed on the Austin trails that young students and couples, clearly not married, spend a lot of time running together—the men often without shirts and the women with little more. They actually look like modern hunters and gatherers, although they run to Whole Foods to scavenge. That doesn't seem quite fair to me when I think of the modern Paleos, the San (bushmen) of the Kalahari, because at Whole Foods the scavenging and hunting and gathering has already been done, and the San start with nothing.

Those seeking better eating and relationships would do well to visit Tuscano. People there eat the Mediterranean diet, and they farm happily, side by side. They live substantially better and longer than the San of the Kalahari, whose hunter/gatherer lifestyle is 40,000 years old. What they did skip, in my observation, were many of the advances in farming of the last 100 years or so. Monsanto was founded in 1901; maybe we should take a harder look at this "progress."

What is the future of marriage without farming in the States? Who knows? I read about a study that showed that divorce rates differ greatly by occupation. A married dancer or bartender is more likely to get divorced—at roughly five times the rate of farmers.

Let's face it, farm families work together, pray together, and go to bed early. Their interaction is limited to socials and church. Bartenders, on the other hand, meet everybody and are often the last resort of those who came to a bar in search of "engagement."

I wouldn't be surprised to learn that urban climates lend themselves to divorce, because there is just so much opportunity for engagement, for making new connections. Dancers engage in close proximity, perhaps scantily clad, with other dancers. A good farmer might call that a bad temptation.

I like the idea of hunting and gathering, for years I thought that is pretty much the same expenditure of time as commuting to work. I felt like I spent the same amount of time in a car that hunter/gatherers spent finding food.

Running and triathlons are a lot of work. Whether they turn out to be a waning fad will depend on the advances in knee and hip replacements. Nevertheless, I lost weight spending my weekends at home in Austin. My wife and I take off to forage for some food at Whole Foods, walking there when the weather permits, as our condo lifestyle requires us to rely on the farming of others.

# 7

# REMEMBER LAKE TRASIMENE

While tourists vary in their approaches to imbibe as fully and freely as possible the treats of a cornucopia like Tuscano, I believe there are bookends to the spectrum. As there is no right answer, I trust no one will be offended by a recitation of the range. There is what I call the Zagat strategy, which is easily characterized and identified. It is the most disciplined extreme. The followers of this orthodoxy can be sighted with all manner of books and maps in and under their arms, and on the tables around them. They began planning their daily, nay hourly, activities six months, three days, and seven hours prior to their departure. They rent a car with a Garmin or a Hertz "almost never lost," and they fight daily "pitched battles," engaging with precision and frontal assaults each and every sight listed in Rick Steve's guide to Italy.

I am nothing like that, and my wife plays along and either tolerates or enjoys my strategy. I am not sure which, and I don't think I will ask. My tourist strategy can only be described as "Fabian" and surely sits on the opposite end of the Zagat strategy.

My Fabian tourist strategy is undisciplined as it begins, and then becomes a game like connect-the-dots. In my humble opinion, as soon as you follow a guide book, you are dealing with secondhand directions—akin to buying a used textbook where someone else has already done highlighting of what they think is important. Guidebooks are pre-highlighted. The origin of the term Fabian, and how I came to rediscover it, could have only happened on a Fabian day.

When you don't rent a car, you tend to walk more,

and you might walk to some places that others think you should drive. On our first full day at Il Falconiere, we decided to make our way up the hill to Cortona. When we asked for directions before leaving, and so much of the conversation was to dissuade us from the attempt, I think we got confused about left and right. In a world of centuries-old windy streets, that only needs to happen once to send you off course greatly. There are no grids, so you can't simply correct your error. And it can take some time, when you are traversing a hillside, to know you are actually moving farther away from the village you are trying to conquer.

Well, we could have gone left or right at our third fork in the country road where we were required to make a decision. As there was no scarecrow to guide us, we followed a street sign that had an arrow that pointed right, which said "Cortona."

That sign, we discovered about an hour and forty-five minutes later, was for cars. Had we gone to the left, which we did the next day, we would have faced a much shorter, but purely vertical, ascent up the Etruscan slope. A better forty-five-minute cardio workout with a view does not exist.

Our ineptly chosen path, though, was a weight-loss meandering journey (worthy of a young Chiana calf) of nearly ten kilometers, which provided frequent vistas of the Valdchiana (the Chiana valley) below. I am certain that the guidebooks and maps would have led us in the other direction—as, when we accompanied someone who had them, that is where they drove.

About an hour into our trek that day, we eyed a body of water, which—were it not a lake—would be the first on the waiting list. In fact, upon arrival in Cortona at the wine shop where we found Palio in the public square, we asked after the ontological status and meaning of the mystic and distant water. We were told it went by the name Lake Trasimene.

We never got closer, nor understood its significance, at that time. In the conversation I heard someone, who was speaking Italian, say "Hannibal."

While I thought that strange, the conversation in Italian was moving like an F1 race car around a circuit, and I didn't quite know what to make of it. I stored the question in midterm memory for a later research session. As it turns out, of course, as with many sights in a place where man- and womankind have lived for thousands of years—there is a story.

The battle of Lake Trasimene, taking place as it did in 217 BC, April or June, depending on whether you follow the Julian or Gregorian Calendar, was fought on the northern shore. This wasn't just any battle. It remains one of the most important and studied battles in the history of humankind. If you have ever been lulled into a situation and experienced surprise, and then felt yourself overcome, you owe the label of that event to Hannibal and the battle of Lake Trasimene.

The birthplace of the military tactic we all know as "ambush" was within our sight as we took the long path upward to Cortona. I can't do justice to the battle or its complete strategic significance, but some highlights are important for the rest of my story. This battle was fought during the Second Punic War, which was the sequel to the First, and the forerunner of the Third.

This set of wars, based on my brief research, was Carthage vs. Rome. The Second Punic War had rock stars, Hannibal and Fabius, in the Italian theatre.

Hannibal invaded Italy from an unlikely and

unexpected point—the Alps. I imagine anyone who could enter Italy that way, in the middle of winter, with three-dozen elephants and mercenaries paid in pillage, would strike fear into the heart of most. And, it appears, Hannibal taunted a traditional Roman tactician, Flaminius, by looting and pillaging and burning country settlements in the region where Cortona sits. And against the counsel of all of his advisors, Flaminius was enraged at Hannibal's defiance and refused to wait for reinforcements.

Upon hearing that Flaminius had broken camp, Hannibal set up an ambush in the wooded hillsides above the lake. The night before the battle, Hannibal had his troops lit campfires in Tuoro to make it look like they were farther away.

In the mist of the morning, Flaminius entered the narrow plain by the lake, and Hannibal's forces ambushed and massacred Flaminius and 15,000 of his troops. Only 6,000 made their way back to Rome.

Like the Alamo inflamed the People's Republic of Texas against Santa Ana, the Battle of Lake Trasimene incited Rome. And, realizing that nothing was between Hannibal and Rome, they suspended the senate and appointed Fabius dictator, with one goal—stop Hannibal.

Being aware of Hannibal's tactical and cavalry superiority, and proven ability to prevail in traditional battles, Fabius engaged in what is now referred to as guerrilla warfare, disrupting supply lines and taking advantage of the fact that Hannibal had to rely on local crops and food sources. Fabius burned crops and food sources in what is now known as scorched earth strategy. His tactics were effective but not respected by his troops or other military leaders. Fabius was replaced by Gauis who returned to traditional strategies. After a humiliating defeat at the Battle of Cannae, the Romans returned to the Fabian strategy and ultimately prevailed. Fabian is known as the "cunctator," which means "delayer," and Fabius is still considered the father of guerrilla warfare and scorched earth strategies.

It didn't end there, of course. George Washington was nicknamed the American Fabius. Sam Houston, after the Alamo, engaged Fabian strategies to annoy Santa Ana while more Texans could be gathered for a great battle. Sam Houston attacked while the Mexicans were enjoying their siesta. How Fabian of him!

That battle ultimately ended the war for Texas. The battle, which took place on my birthday, April 21st, was called the battle of San Jacinto, and coincidentally is the name of the street I live on in Austin. On my birthday every year, San Jacinto Day is celebrated as an "independence day" in Texas.

As I glanced at a lake in Italy and then flew back to our home in Austin, Texas, I realized I was going home in my mind. I felt the tie. It's my roots now. I realized I'm a Texan.

But this realization all began on the plains below Cortona at Lake Trasimene, which I only discovered on an opportune walk.

# 8

## BANCAROTTA, WHAT IS OLD IS NEW AGAIN

We live for a time on this earth. And if we live long enough, we see patterns and repetitions. And we learn more from experiencing them than we do from reading about them. Business cycles are one such example of a recurring phenomenon. Every six or seven years, it seems there is a bubble or an adjustment after a period of gains, an uptick after a downtick; it goes by many names.

Extraordinary upheavals are less common. Unless you live for over 100 years, it is unlikely you would experience two depressions, for example. The Great Depression was launched with the stock market crash in 1929. And while technically the Great Recession started in 2007, Lehman crashed around September 15, 2008. Both these were led by the massive failure of financial institutions. We forget about them until a major event—something so horrible that it somehow earns the label "Great"—whacks us upside our collective heads. And the Great Recession was a worldwide phenomenon. Countries such as Italy are still feeling the aftershocks.

As my roots tend toward country, and dark and dank museums make me yearn for sunshine and God's earlier creations, I gravitate to the open air and verdant landscape. Nevertheless, one can't resist the necessity of touring through at least Firenze and Siena, if for no other reason than to avoid the gapes and gasps upon your return of the *cognoscenti* who will otherwise surely hold you in contempt for your failure. In support of this notion, my wife and I spent a half-day in each, so we could nod "of course" when the question arises, as it has already.

## Bancarotta, What is Old is New Again

Don't misunderstand me, buildings like The Duomo in Siena are beautiful and stunning, and often hold frescos and statues. The primary wonder for me is "How did they do that so perfectly with the tools of the craft available at the time?"

I felt that way as I encountered a building that had a grand statue of a large and esteemed ancient gentleman in front, but looked like a federal reserve bank building in New York or San Francisco. You know the edifice—strong stoned, symmetrically fortified, as if to say, "What is inside stays inside, and what is outside stays outside." The sign says, "Do not enter, do not pass go, do not collect $200." In short, I was in the presence of a bank.

Banks are important places, holding our fortunes and our dreams. That is why they look as imposing as cathedrals. God and mammon share one characteristic. That is, the need to look you in the eye and say, "I am bigger and stronger than you." And this was not any bank I was viewing; it was the oldest bank in the world, founded in 1472. Yes—Monte dei Paschi, the third-largest bank in Italy, is the oldest bank in the world. And, like younger banks in the US and elsewhere, it appears to have engaged in undisclosed derivative trades, requiring a bailout by a country itself the subject of a bailout.

Just prior to our arrival, in January 2013, the bank had gotten a €3.9 billion emergency loan from Italy. The history of the entire region encompassing Siena and Firenze seems tied up with financial matters and families—and a family name associated with Firenze pops into every conversation of the city's glorious and artistic and financial past, the Medicis.

An essay of this duration does not permit an epoch on the rise and fall of the Medici family empire. But, suffice it to say, these folks knew how to manage and lend money, and they did so for nearly 100 years from 1397–1494. They were early pioneers of debits and credits, the double-entry accounting system.

The father of the fatherland himself, Cosimo, is one of those folks you would pick, if you could pick anyone to have dinner with, as he surely accelerated humanism by founding three libraries in Florence and having the works of Plato translated from Greek to Latin, giving the Florentines access to someone besides Aristotle.

# Bancarotta, What is Old is New Again

Their failure came as the result of what makes banks fail—lending to the wrong folks. In the case of the Medicis, their downfall began when they started to lend to secular leaders to help finance wars. Edward IV basically bankrupted the London branch when he couldn't repay the loans after the Wars of the Roses. It didn't help that the London branch had also loaned money to the opposition.

I can't quite fathom a family being the wealthiest family in Europe and loaning globally during such a pre-electronic time. My closest understanding of family banking is much more humble, but just as interesting in its own way.

My wife's ancestors had a family bank for many years in a small town in western Missouri, a farmers bank. The Thomas family bank, sold just a few years before the Great Recession, actually survived the Great Depression. The story of how it did is told to all the descendants as they meet for holidays. I have heard the story many times—so gracious and humble apologies if I get it not just right to my dear friends and the Thomas family.

Word of bank collapse and failure reached the small town of Mound City, Missouri. A line had formed outside of the Exchange Bank. Great-Grandpa Thomas faced what all bankers faced, the potential for a run on the bank. And as all understand by now, banks don't have the money you entrust to them; they loan it to others. He held off the customers by saying he needed to go to Kansas City and would be back. He took a big briefcase with him, and everyone watched him board the train. He returned, as I believe I heard, the next day, and was confronted by, among others, the richest man in Mound City.

Great-Grandpa Thomas said to all, "The Exchange Bank is fine and open for business. Anyone who wants their money can have it."

All stared at the briefcase, presuming it was full of money. The richest man in town looked at the briefcase and at Great-Grandpa Thomas, and said, "I am keeping my money in the bank, right where it is."

The line dispersed, and the bank survived. Years later, the story goes, he was asked what was in the brief-case. "Well, my dirty socks" was his reply.

Maybe Great-Grandpa Thomas could have helped the Medicis.

# 9

# IT'S A SMALL WORLD
# AFTER ALL

aving the good fortune to be born with loving parents under modest circumstances, I recall clearly the special treats in life. Though I was born in Philadelphia, I spent my "Wonder Bread" years—ages five to twelve—in Pittsburgh. As it was the sixties, steel mills spewing sulfur and the associated smells were part of my "christening." As money was measured in our family by cents and not dollars, small treats were a big deal. An occasional trip to McDonald's—where I savored the Big Mac with an order of large fries and a strawberry milkshake, a twice-a-year visit to Isaly's for ice cream in Pittsburgh; and a trip to a Pirates game—where, if you were under eighteen, you could sit in the bleachers for a dollar—were among my treasured childhood treats.

But there was a magical trip we took once by car to a magical place on the occasion of the New York World's Fair in 1962. I was three years old. I recall being overcome with wonder at the larger-than-life characters. The one ride stuck in my head with the associated song. That song, almost annoyingly repetitive, returned to my consciousness one day in Tuscano.

In a world of social media and human "virtuality" and disconnected connections—see e.g., http://lifeatlarge.us/ by Chris Sibley, et al., coproduced by yours truly, et al. ("a dramedy about a recluse who lives online until he meets someone that teaches him about a world greater than the World Wide Web")—I suppose connecting without the Internet is an archaic science, bordering on alchemy. It is possible that someday meeting without the Internet will be a lost art celebrated in nostalgic musicals similar to *Meet me in St Louis*.

As trends portend this sad future, I thought I would begin to record, humbly, some tips for the strangers of the future on how to connect without benefit of the Internet with those you may find engaging, those who challenge and complement your world view, and those who kindle your soul. The secret is secret places.

Il Falconiere is such a secret place. It sits slightly above the valley in Tuscano where whales once played. The Baracchi family has made this estate their home for several centuries. The current custodians of the elegant estate are Riccardo Baracchi, a Tuscan's Tuscan, and his beautiful wife, Silvia. They are best friends with Frances Mayes, who visited with us on our second day there. She was the author of *Under the Tuscan Sun: At Home in Italy.* The Villa Bramasole in a nearby village was made famous by her book, and the movie of the same name.

We had seen the movie based on her book at least a dozen times. We own a copy. It was what inspired us to make this trip to Toscano in the first place. Mayes still lives in Cortona at least half of the year, and she had popped in for a wine tasting.

Riccardo explained to me that the word Bramasole meant a "yearning for the sun."

The following day, I asked Riccardo what he thought of the Antinori, Bramasole, a fine 2007 Syrah we had tasted in Cortona. Riccardo said that it was rated 85, while his Syrah was rated 94. I was glad I didn't have to make those decisions. More importantly, he added that Frances was still quite upset with Piero Antinori, as he did not call her to ask her permission to use the name of her villa for his wine. Tuscan tension exists.

At that moment, my mind traveled back to Chicago in the nineties when I met Italian wine-maker Piero Antinori. At the time, I represented restaurants such as Carlucci's, which carried his wines. I was so impressed with Piero. He had what I think of as European charisma—an old-world style. I could almost see the family features in the face, the look of royalty—the look of distinctiveness and distinction, not perfection. He at once looked like his ancestors, and yet he was there speaking with that old-world accent, in flawless English. Mesmerizing. I was so impressed and taken by his features, language, and style, I put the story about meeting him in my book *StagNation*. Piero had told me then how his family had been in the wine business for more than 600 years—that people in Europe were virtually immobile, and didn't easily or often leave their ancestral homeland.

My own life was in sharp contrast to Piero's, one might even say Fabian. I slaved at the time, as all did at a large Chicago law firm, Jenner & Block. I missed the last train to the suburbs too many times with a double Bombay and tonic in hand to ease the 12:30 a.m. milk run that was stuffed with accountants, lawyers, and investment bankers, all working to achieve the keys to the executive washroom, also known as partnership.

At Jenner, one of the great lawyers I worked for was Howard Barron. A more gentlemanly lawyer I doubt you could meet. Howard had gone to a junior college— at least that is what it said on his wall, Stanford Leland Junior College—and then Yale Law School. When our son, Andrew Cash, was born, Howard sent us a silver spoon, which we cherish to this day. Though we were still friends, I hadn't seen Howard in years.

Sipping my wine in Cortona, I thought wistful- ly about Piero, and my days in Chicago representing restaurants—and my friends and lawyers at the firm, including my friend Howard.

At Il Falconiere, that secret place, we met so many secret people. These are treats of a different sort. We met Benjamin and his beautiful wife, Jay, from Puerto Rico on their honeymoon—he a one-time chef at Gramercy Tavern in New York, now having returned to his homeland in Puerto Rico and married to Jay, a recent graduate of medical school and also a native Puerto Rican. She would be doing her residence at the veterans hospital in San Juan, which was too busy these days. They explained that, as residents of a US territory, Puerto Ricans are called first to serve in wartime. I didn't know that.

On our last night at Il Falconiere, we shared a dinner with Don and Jeannett. Don was an employment lawyer who had just finished a ten-year stint as mayor of Coral Gables, Florida. They were celebrating their forty-fourth anniversary. He had some fun stories that included Prince Albert of Monaco.

Jeff and Tanya from Sonoma, celebrating their thirtieth anniversary, hailed from the Bay Area, and would now likely be lifelong friends. We made plans to see them in Sienna the next day—we were moving to a hotel near Firenze. And then we would see them in Sonoma mid-June where I was planning to finish my next book, *BOOMERangs: Engaging the Aging Workforce in America,* a book about the need for change in attitudes and laws to align them with our changing demographics.

Four Texans from Houston (having been in Texas ten years, I can pick Texans out of a crowd—and Texans from Houston are particularly easy) celebrating their sixtieth birthdays rounded out the guests—but for four folk from Chicago.

"Where are you from?" may be the most oft-heard phrase in places like Il Falconiere. I heard it more than *buongiorno*. The four folks from Chicago sipping Sangiovese, clearly a couple and their parents, had asked us the day before, "Where are you from?"

We said Austin and Dallas, Texas. Their Chicago accent indicated pure Lake Shore heritage. Seeing an easy and comfortable path to enlightened engagement, we shared that we had lived in Chicago.

As the conversation deepened, we got to, "What did you do there?"

When I mentioned Jenner & Block, the eldest of the four, Tom, asked, "Did you know Howard Barron?"

I was stunned again and happily shared that Howard was a dear friend.

I talked about the work I had done in mergers and acquisitions for Howard and his client, Continental Grain Company. Tom smiled and said, "I play bridge with Howard every Thursday."

There I was, in the middle of nowhere on a cloudy day in the Tuscan hills—a place where I'd least expect to know anyone, or run into anything familiar; and here was a man who would have the pleasure of my friend Howard's company in just two days. I was envious. I wished I could see my friend on Thursday!

We shared some wine and Howard stories as the sun finally peaked in through the clouds. It was a *Bramasole* moment.

As Evie and I walked off to soak in the Etruscan spa, the Disney song from my childhood invaded the Tuscan stillness.

By way of disclosure, not one of the guests had found Il Falconiere on the Internet. All said it was recommended by a friend or travel agent who had been there. I fear, now that we have left, that Il Falconiere may be like Brigadoon, and only appear for a brief period every hundred years.-

## It's A Small World After All

I know it wasn't just the place—it was the combination—the secret place and the secret people there
that led to the magic.

# 10

# GOD BLESS THE BASTARD, HIS MOTHER, AND A PHILADELPHIA LAWYER

obbies and habits developed while abroad have varying half-lives, I suppose. Commitments made to continue activities launched overseas are not much stronger than New Year's resolutions. And so I wondered whether my essay writing would survive the transition from the lush landscapes of Tuscano to the less inspiring world of Texas Urbana.

This final essay will show that, at least a month later, my essay writing continued. It wasn't the rolling hills of the Texas Hill Country nor the California Sonoma wine country, which I visited shortly after, that triggered this essay, but a kind comment from a neighbor who read many of the essays and a simple cemetery in Southlake, Texas, at White's Chapel.

My friend Walter wrote me a note, saying that my essays were "Nickersonian." I wondered where that "sonian" term emanated. The word "Smithsonian," popped into my head—I do not know why. So I had a chance to do some quick research on the topic and was fascinated to find some amazing facts and a tie-in to a cemetery in Genoa, Italy.

Cemeteries in the United States, like the simple cemetery in Southlake, our hometown for our first ten years in Texas, show a lack of respect for the dead, if judged by Italian standards. On the second tier of that Etruscan hillside upon which Cortona sits, there is a glorious cemetery honoring the departed souls of the region. Each crypt, each tomb, each walled memorial is more ornate than the last. Clear pictures of the former denizens of Cortona guarded their remains. Fresh flowers adorned the aged concrete, even for those who had not walked the earth for 100 years. There is an abundance of respect and honor; a dignified coliseum.

I felt so much respect, I was not drawn to my camera to capture it. Couldn't.

And I imagined that the grave of John Smithson, namesake of the esteemed Smithsonian Institution in Washington DC, was grand before the city of Genoa, Italy, contacted the United States when they wanted to move the cemetery where Smithson's remains were honored.

As you drink your coffee this morning, you might thank—or at least think of—James Smithson. James Smithson was a scientist who wrote twenty-seven scientific papers in his lifetime. He believed that science was the greatest calling of humankind, and the key to happiness. The subjects of his papers were diverse, ranging from the chemistry of volcanoes, to methods for improving the making of coffee, to the contents of a "lady's tear." He never married, nor fathered children. He dedicated his life to science and scientific inquiry. He wandered through Europe, collecting ores and minerals, with a special interest in carbonates. Zinc carbonate, now known as smithsonite, is named after him.

His father was the Duke of Northumberland, a man of tremendous wealth. His mother was a widow, and a cousin of the Duchess of Northumberland. As James's parents lacked the Church's blessing on their brief "union," his mother had to go to Paris to have the child. That is where James was born in 1765.

The exact date of his birth is unknown, because, if one were a bastard back then, nobody was supposed to know you were born. And we should never have heard of James Smithson, nor known the name James Smithson, in that he never came to the United States, alive at least, save for one simple, incredible fact and mysterious feat.

James Smithson, that Oxford-educated bastard, left more than 100,000 gold sovereigns to the United States of America in his will, subject to the condition that his nephew die without heirs (so we have his nephew to thank as well).

In Smithson's will, the final draft of which was signed on October 23, 1826 (I read it in his own handwriting), he left his entire estate, with the aforementioned condition, "to the United States of America to found at Washington, under the name to the Smithsonian Institution, an establishment for the increase and diffusion of knowledge among men."

Nobody knows why he did this, and there is not even consistent speculation. The United States didn't even know about the bequeathment until years later in 1835.

The great Philadelphia lawyer, Richard Rush, was sent to England in 1836 by President Andrew Jackson to fetch what amounted to a true treasure, eleven boxes of gold sovereigns. After two years and a successful lawsuit in Chancery in England, Richard Rush brought the gold home to the US.

Here I must digress—a two-year lawsuit in Chancery Court? I must confess that I remember vividly the fictional case of Jarndyce v. Jarndyce from Bleak House. Charles Dickens in the very first chapter depicts with prosaic grace the worthlessness and uselessness of the Court of Chancery in 1852—how nothing could get done.

"Jarndyce v Jarndyce drones on. This scarecrow of a suit has, in course of time, become
so complicated that no man alive knows what
it means. The parties to it understand it least,
but it has been observed that no two Chancery lawyers can talk about it for five minutes
without coming to a total disagreement as to
all the premises. Innumerable children have
been born into the cause; innumerable old
people have died out of it. Scores of persons
have deliriously found themselves made parties in Jarndyce v Jarndyce without knowing
how or why; whole families have inherited
legendary hatreds with the suit. The little
plaintiff or defendant who was promised a
new rocking-horse when Jarndyce v Jarndyce
should be settled has grown up, possessed
himself of a real horse, and trotted away into
the other world. Fair wards of court have faded
into mothers and grandmothers; a long proces-
sion of Chancellors has come in and gone out;
the legion of bills in the suit have been transformed into mere bills of mortality; there are

not three Jarndyces left upon the earth perhaps
since old Tom Jarndyce in despair blew his
brains out at a coffeehouse in Chancery Lane;
but Jarndyce v Jarndyce still drags its dreary
length before the court, perennially hopeless."

So, consider the feat. In just two years, Richard
Rush rescued the gold that made possible the revered
Smithsonian Institution, which, through April of 2013,
was estimated to have had 9.6 million visitors. Now
that's a Philadelphia lawyer!

But it was not over yet, Congress had to argue for
eight years over whether to accept it or not—and if ac-
cepted, what should be done with it? Congress debated
and debated, using most of the airtime as a way to curse
the British for all they had done. As education was a
matter for the states under the constitution, John C.
Calhoun of South Carolina, among others, was con-
cerned about enlarging federal power. While Congress
argued for eight years about the funds (amounting to
over $500,000) 1/66th of the federal budget at the time,
and about equal to Harvard's then endowment, were

invested in the bonds of a new state, Arkansas, and promptly disappeared when the state defaulted three years after the investment.

I suppose nothing really changes.

Congress voted to replace the funds in 1842. This must have broken Rush's heart as when he was Treasury secretary under Adams from 1825–1829, he paid off the federal debt. The Smithsonian was eventually created by an Act of Congress in 1846 (signed by President James K. Polk).

Smithson did eventually make his way to the United States. His remains were retrieved from Genoa, Italy, in 1904, where he had been laid to rest, when the Genoan's decided to move the cemetery. Who retrieved the remains? Alexander Graham Bell himself, an early regent of the institution.

The money had not been earned by Smithson. He inherited it from his mother, Elizabeth Hungerford Keate Macie, a wealthy widow.

Whatever motives Smithson had, to the extent he articulated them, burned with his papers in a fire at the Smithsonian in 1865. You can read about it in Harper's.

But I think it is interesting to look at what was happening in 1826 in the USA, when he made his will.

Both John Adams and Thomas Jefferson died on July 4, 1826, the fiftieth anniversary of the signing of the Declaration of Independence. This news surely reached Smithson in Italy by October of that year. The United States surely looked like a land of opportunity, where 100,000 gold sovereigns could really make a difference—and it has. Thanks to a bastard, his mother, and a Philadelphia lawyer—with no help from Congress.

When we complete a major deal or task in our business lives, it is considered a "best practice" to have a "lessons learned" meeting and discuss what went well and what did not, so as to improve upon the performance in the future. With a trip like my Tuscan adventure, it is not quite so simple, because one person left on the trip and another returned. I left a vacationer, a person desiring to see, taste, smell, and imbibe the elements of the Tuscan experience. I returned with a new world-view, a view that understands and sees connections between seemingly unrelated things. Some might call it a religious experience. Humanists would say I reached a new level of understanding. If you tend toward spirituality and fate, you might like Albert Einstein's quote: "Coincidence is God's way of remaining anonymous." I am fine with that. But I also believe there is a code behind the things we see, and mostly we are just satisfied with it—like the set of a movie.

As a former philosophy major at Carleton College in Northfield, Minnesota, I recall from memory Plato's Cave analogy, the gist of which is that prisoners are watching shadows on a cave wall and not seeing the things themselves. One prisoner is unchained and sees the actual things that are causing the shadows, and understands the difference. The prisoner leaves the cave and sees the sun, and understands its role. Finally, the prisoner returns to the cave to enlighten those who are still watching shadows.

I had too many "coincidences" to call them mere "coincidences." I see levers and pulleys I never thought of before, and tumblers of interrelated locks. And notwithstanding Plato's cave analogy, I am confident it is a process, not a destination. One needs to go back and forth from the cave to the sun.

So I shall return to the Tuscan sun in the fall for the harvest, with my eyes and mind more open and wider. Maybe I will take a copy of Plato's Republic with me this time and visit the Medici Chapel and thank them for providing safe haven to the Greeks fleeing the Turks, and launching the Renaissance with the introduction of Plato to Italy in Florence. I guess you could say I had my own personal renaissance in Central Italy.

I can't wait to "retorno."

# ABOUT THE AUTHOR

A uthor, businessman, and philanthropist, Cash Nickerson, is president and CFO of PDS Tech, Inc., the fourth-largest engineering and Information Technology staffing firm in the United States. He has held a variety of legal and executive positions in his career, including serving as an attorney and marketing executive for Union Pacific Railroad and as an associate and then partner at Jenner & Block, one of Chicago's five largest law firms. He founded a human resources company, Workforce Strategies, which he sold in three years for high seven figures and later founded an Internet company he took public through a reverse merger. Nickerson holds a JD and MBA from Washington University in St. Louis where he was an editor of the law review and a recipient of the US Steel Scholarship.

Nickerson is actively licensed to practice law in Texas, California, Illinois, Nevada, and Nebraska. He received the Global Philanthropy Award in 2010 from Washington University in St. Louis for his support of the Crimes Against Humanity Initiative and is a member of the Law School National Council. He is an avid martial artist, ranked as a third degree black belt in Kenpo Karate, as well as being a Russian Martial Arts instructor. His first book, StagNation: Understanding the New Normal in Employment, was published in 2013. He lives with his wife Evie in Austin, Texas.

Visit Cash at http://cashnickerson.com/

# COMING SOON

## Crashing Wings
### Path Notes from a Texan Martial Artist

## A Texan's Return to Tuscany
### The Falcon becomes the Falconer